CW00549821

BERNINI'S CAT

GERDA MAYER

NEW & SELECTED POEMS

First Published 1999 by IRON Press
5 Marden Terrace
Cullercoats
North Shields
Northumberland NE30 4PD UK
Tel/Fax (0191) 253 1901

Typeset in Garamond 10pt by Annette Whitfield
Printed by Peterson Printers South Shields

Cover design by Michael Adam & Peter Mortimer
Cover Moggy by Richard Jardine
Book design by Peter Mortimer

ISBN: 0 906228 69 7

FIRST EDITION

IRON Press Books are represented by
Signature Book Representation
Sun House, 2 Little Peter Street
Manchester M15 4PS
Tel: (0161) 834 8767
Fax: (0161) 834 8656

e-mail: signatur@dircon.co.uk

northern
arts
PROMOTING THE ARTS
IN THE NORTH

Gerda Mayer (née Stein) was born in Karlsbad, Czechoslovakia in 1927, and came to England at the age of eleven, in 1939. She was educated at schools in Dorset and Surrey, and, in her thirties (1960–63), at Bedford College, University of London. After leaving school, she did landwork for seventeen months in Worcestershire and Surrey, and then office work in London. She married Adolf Mayer in 1949. She has published several collections of verse, and her poems have been widely anthologised in the U.K. and other countries.

Acknowledgements are due to
Gerda Mayer's previous collections

Gerda Mayer's Library Folder, (7 poems ill. by Deirdre Farrell, All-in 1972.)
Treble Poets 2, (Chatto & Windus, 1975.)
The Knockabout Show, London, (Chatto & Windus, 1978.)
*Monkey on the Analyst's Couch, (Ceolfrith Press, 1980.)
The Candyfloss Tree, (Oxford University Press, 1984.)
March Postman, (Priapus Press, 1985.)
A Heartache of Grass, (Peterloo Poets, 1988.)
Time Watching, (Hearing Eye, 1995.)

* *A Poetry Book Society recommendation.*

and to the following magazines and anthologies in which
some of the poems first appeared

*Ambit; Ambit Festschrift; And; Anthology of Little Magazine Poets,
Asylum Publications; Country Life; Doors; Encounter; Gallery;
Gown Literary Supplement; The Honest Ulsterman; Jewish Quarterly; Kudos;
Manifold; New Poetry 1; New Statesman; The Observer; Omnibus; Ore; Other Poet
The Oxford Treasury of Children's Poems; Palantir; Pink Peace;
Poetry and Audience; Poetry Durham; Poetry Matters; Poetry Quartely;
The Poetry Review; Rialto; Samphire; The Spectator; Tagus;
The First Lick of the Lolly; The Green Book; Through a Window; Time Haiku; Tub
What on Earth...?; Workshop New Poetry.*

CONTENTS

1950s

Narcissus 9
In His Orchard 10
Still Life: Rose on a Polished Table . 11

1960s

The Peach 15
Unseen 16
Nocturne 1 17
The Man on the Desert Island (1) . 18
Small Park in East Germany 19
They Went 20
Imagism 21
Lorelei 22
The Love Message 23
Seen in Regent's Park 24
Aesthetes 25
Bernini's Cat 26
Star Of Sorrow 27
Sound Judgement 28
Man Takes a Bite.
Man Takes Another Bite 29

1970s

Coming up for Air 33
Salutation to Karl Marx 34
Visa for a Return Visit Refused 35
Punch and Judy Show 36
In the Open Air Restaurant 37
The Agnostic's Prayer 38
Song 39

Eat it all up, Darlings 40
Tales 41
Fragment 42
Paper Boat 43
Bang 44
Toad 45
The Birthright 46
Three Autumns in Regent's Park . . 47
A Lion, a Wolf and a Fox 48
Old Mrs Lazibones 49
Shallow Poem 50
The Knockabout Show 51
All The Leaves Have Lost
Their Trees 52
Lullaby 53
A Matter Of Taste 54
Hide and Seek 56
Sage 57
Basho Tries Again 58
X Marx the Spot 58
Dandelions 58
To a Conker 59
The Inheritor 60
White Lamplight 61
Farewell 62
Time Watching 63
House Moving 64
The Man on the Desert
Island (5) 65
Noah 66

1970s (continued)

Esmeralda 67

Dull Town... 68

God Wot 69

W. H. Auden 70

My Own, My Native Land. 71

For Tommy. 72

The Lodger. 74

Carve me up when I Die 75

1980s

The Poetry Reading. 79

Anon 80

Mrs K's Letter. 81

The Poet Reclining 82

On a Sheet of Formica:
An Incantation. 83

Make Believe 84

Lines Written in High Darren,
Llanigan, Near Hay-on-Wye, 1980 . 85

The Seven. 86

The Crunch 87

Poplar 87

Male Butterflies
Court Falling Leaves 88

Confetti 89

Owl. 90

Children with Candles 90

Grandfather's House. 91

The Fart of an Angel. 92

Once. 93

Absorbed 94

Cinderella's Slipper 95

The Emigration Game — Winter
1938/39. 96

Mirrors. 97

At Night 97

Stock Still. 98

Stumped. 99

Dullard-the-mind:
Sluggard-the-body 100

Swimmer's Song 101

Gipsy Song (Translation) 102

1990s

Hunger. 105

Malham Tarn Field Centre -
Yorkshire, 1992. 106

Two Haiku. 106

The Misanthrope's Baby Poem . . . 107

Kaffee und Kuchen 108

NARCISSUS

What he liked in her voice
was his name
called over & over
and the mirrorlike look
in the weeping eyes of his lover;
in the end, left her
on a chill mountain shelf,
in a damp cave
with her wits and her words astray,
to devote himself
to himself.

Then the gods with indolent yawns
took a high hand with him for
such eNOR
mous self-love
was considered by others a bore.

Changed to a flower
he stood by the river
a sad case
of rooted vanity;
he never forgave
the reflecting water
for rippling his face.

IN HIS ORCHARD

In his orchard of little ripe corpses
The giant walked one day
And the little wind in the branches
Carried the stench away:

Carried it over the fencing
Of skeletons linking arms,
Where Lieschen and Gretchen were dawdling,
Surveying the orchard's charms.

They did not weep for the dead men
Bobbing in the trees,
They did not weep for their hungry eyes,
They did not weep for these.

They were nice, blonde, natural girls,
And when the smell arose
From where the giant was striding,
Each giggled and held her nose.

Between dances and beer that evening,
Said Gretchen, raising her drink:
No wonder he had to hang them;
They absolutely stink.

STILL LIFE: ROSE ON A POLISHED TABLE

Like a long-legged golden lady
Stands the dark rose in a glitter of glass;
Like a poised woman with a small white wrist
Moving in tinkling sun and laughter shadows,
Cool luxuries and summer indolence,
Stands the dark rose; bends a little
Over the gold-glow pool of the table,
As if her silken fragrance looks to find
An answering ripple of red petal and rose.

THE PEACH

My fairy ill-wishers
cast a sour eye
on my father's raptures
on my mother's lullaby.

Let her be socially inept,
let her wear a plain face.
(Youth conspired briefly
to camouflage my disgrace.)

Let lover and beloved
seldom meet in one person.
And my blabbing tongue too
they put a curse on.

But one, with more finesse,
gave me the peach
that hangs on the high branch
barely out of reach.

Barely out of reach it hangs,
the almost-to-be-had:
my evil spirits squat around
and watch me hopping mad.

UNSEEN

Present met Past,
Said: I am your Future.
But Past walked by
Without look or gesture.

Present then strained
To define Past's nature,
But his sight was too short
To catch every feature.

While Present looked back
Absorbed in the creature
Future walked by;
Unseen; without gesture.

NOCTURNE 1

The dark rain flutters through the trees,
Through my unsleep. The dark rain
Plucks the strings of the dustbin-lid.
                            Softly
It seeps under my kneecap, beneath
My knuckles. Not pain. An awareness.
I lie awake with the rain and the small
                            rheumatics of love.

THE MAN ON THE DESERT ISLAND (1)

The man on the desert island
Has forgotten the ways of people,
His stories are all of himself.
Day in, day out of time
He communes with himself and sends
Messages in green bottles:
Help me they say *I am*
Cast up and far from home.
Each day he goes to watch
The horizon for ships.
Nothing reaches his shore
Except corked green bottles.

SMALL PARK IN EAST GERMANY

Crumbling and weathered, their features half- erased,
they stand gracefully in these gardens under the quiet sun,
satyrs and goddesses, some in niches of leaves;
now they're returning to stone, they are more real
than when - what ages ago? - they were wheeled in
and put up, looking too white and too newly chiselled.

Once all was gay and decorous; children white-beribboned
and sailor-suited drove their hoops before them, the white
whipped cream topped aromatic coffee, and the band
played in the open air to the prosperous and the bourgeois.

The band is silent, the café locked up, the too
prosperous have departed. And departed too is
that later and crooked time that fouled Germany's air.
Now is the time of unyielding ideals; the egalitarian
walk here but without conviction and feel out of place.

But whose place was it ever? The happy complacent
once owned it perhaps but in a different way;
then came the blackly hysterical, then the quietly out-of-sorts.
It seems to belong to itself and is growing towards Arcadia;
a half-forgotten garden full of dense leaves and sun,
and nymphs and satyrs breaking from weathered stone.

THEY WENT

My father went hiking without pass-
port or visa and was
                              intercepted
My sister went mad my mother
went into that Chamber trusting
                              in God
God picked the bones clean they lie
without imprint or name dear
                              mother

IMAGISM

poems like lace
patterned around
pauses

winter twigs
holding light

LORELEI

Lorelei, the story has it
You are sitting on some rocks,
And alluring and in-luring
Combing out your golden locks.

But the story misses out on
What you're really doing there;
You're assessing your reflection,
As you rearrange your hair.

And those suicides by water,
Though of course they gratify,
Whilst you wait for Captain Right, are
Mere fringe benefits, Lorelei.

THE LOVE MESSAGE

To Lotus
her lover, the poet,
sends a branch of
white blossom,
posting the branch
down the river:
& from the river
she plucks it
& interleaving
her hair with
flowers
flaunts them
(to make
the other girls
round-eyed).
When the flowers
are wilted, Lotus
will strip the
branch, making
a stick to
prop her old age.
VANITY
CAN'T LAY ASIDE
OLD COMPLIMENTS.

SEEN IN REGENT'S PARK

Tall, stork-like, he
Stalks on the tall lawn,
The man-sized bird,

Stretching his legs:
Five steps, turns;
Five steps and turns

Again; humbled,
Held in by
Invisible bars.

Did Fury once
Fight those bars?
Agony plead? Did Despair

Throw itself against them?
Did he grow cunning
then, watching for

A weakness? And then
Rational, saying
These things are

Inanimate. Let us
Reason our way out?
Did his dreams,

And only his dreams,
Bend the bars
To an escape?

The bars are gone now.
The bars confine him.
· Iron experience

Became iron habit.
Tall, stork-like, he stalks
On the tall lawn,

Five paces. Turns.

AESTHETES

Behind December branches
Stand the blue angels of dusk
With apricot wings

Under their darkling hands
All things are ennobled
The trivialities
Like garden gnomes
Vanish on the heels of day

Dusk and
Marigold lamplight
And luminous flights of cars
And I a dark shape moving
My spirit cold and complaining

But cold hands or glowing faces
Love or isolation
The angels say
Are none of their concern

As carefully in the pale sky
They fix a sickle moon

BERNINI'S CAT

The tabby, in front of
electric bars,
having his chin scratched, feigns
St Teresa's ecstasy:
head back,
eyes closed,
mouth open. O
Heaven!

star is it ? it is the star of sorrow

what a star

star of

it is the star of

you on our arms

on israel

it has shone for a long time

night we wear

Star of sorrow
Star of a dark night
We wear you on our arms

What star is it?
It is the star of Israel
It has shone for a long time

SOUND JUDGEMENT

Of two appletrees in my garden
One bears sound fruit but dull;
The other's apples are
Maggoty and sweet.

If you had to choose
I ask a friend
Which would you rather be?

The sweet and maggoty apple
Replies my dull but sound friend.

MAN TAKES A BITE.
MAN TAKES ANOTHER BITE.

A maggot found an apple;
A sweet round apple;
Green as grass, sound as paradise.
The maggot bit into the apple
And straightway was filled with a heady need
To thrust his way into the core of that fruit,
Into its inmost heart; to explore
The ends and bounds of it. The maggot
Fell in love with the apple and sang
'Apple, green apple,' - as he nibbled away its skin.

And as the apple diminished, so the maggot grew;
He curled right round the apple; his eyes
Saw his tail; his portion advancing
Saw his portion receding. Each day,
The apple grew smaller, the maggot grew more obese.
The maggot then grieved for the apple's decline.
'Apple, green apple,' he sang and wept
Cider tears (he was so full of it).
The apple then fell to the ground, having grown very frail.
The maggot grew wings and flew to another apple.

Small, hard, indigestible.

COMING UP FOR AIR

Homecoming
is often
not what we have expected.

Rip Van Winkle awakes:
an old man &
outlandish.

Take Orwell's hero:
'coming up for air'
he finds a depletion of oxygen;

And Mann's Tonio
is almost arrested;-
he of the town's First.

Only his dog
knew Ulysses. Strangers
live in my house.

Often
homecoming is not
what we have expected.

Is this jigsaw
my town? Only
some of the pieces fit.

NOTE: In Thomas Mann's short novel "Tonio Kroger",
Tonio who belonged to one of the Town's leading families,
draws suspicion on himself when he revisits his home town.

SALUTATION TO KARL MARX

Between the round municipal flowerbeds
(Chocolate-drops sprinkled with hundreds-and-thousands)
Squats Karl Marx as heavy as a dull book,
If a bust can be said to squat, and so I hail him here,
My one co-religionist in this German town.
Well met? Ill met? Let us say - oddly encountered,
In Karl Marx Street, no less; what once may have been
Siegheil-or Judenraus Strasse - and might be again.
For Fate can make Charlies of us, who now puts us up
With some courtesy. She may cart us off
(Having done so, often before). Wherefore, here today,
Pulling your metaphorical leg, I salute you:
Partly in earnest - seeing the moment is transient.

VISA FOR A RETURN VISIT REFUSED

An official in Prague tosses a pin into the air;
a small rusty pin, slightly bent, and it lands on NO;
and *no* he cables back to my supplication for a visa.

The trees of Bohemia fall into line and march away;
further and further they recede and smaller and darker,
a distancing army of ants; then snow; a blankness of snow.

PUNCH AND JUDY SHOW

Bastard and Bitch lived in a house,
One had a grudge, the other a grouse;
Grouse and Grudge lived side by side,
Though doors and windows were open wide.

Was it sex, that cur, that kept them together?
Or the visibly querulous weather?
Lethargy, was it? or expectation
That through their front door would walk Salvation,

Goodlooking, impeccable, endlessly kind,
To make off with Himher, leaving Herhim behind?
Acrimonious fidelity is not so uncommon,
Time grieved them grey, the man and the woman;-

Knocker and Scold, knocked out, made hoarse,
And the onlookers well-entertained of course.
Fold up the booth, pack in the scene,
The moon comes out, and the tide flows in.

IN THE OPEN AIR RESTAURANT

The waiter licks the tablecloth clean
he licks clean the plates the glasses the
flowers his tongue
moves between the prongs of the forks
he shows his guests to the table they order
      tongue
            His
    moves
           delicately
over the young girl's neck

THE AGNOSTIC'S PRAYER

God, to whom I'm still inclined to
say my prayers, though God knows why,
guard me, if you have a mind to,
while I here abandoned lie.

I depend on your good nature.
Irony leads me astray.
Save the world, God, save your creatures,
save us for a rainy day.

Thank you for your grace and favour,
though the memory's remote.
Keep my cat safe, keep my neighbour's,
keep them from each other's throat.

SONG

Go to sleep, for upstairs
cross-eyed God is answering prayers,
and replies
to your sighs
with solace made for others' cares.

Go to sleep, on your shores
still a summer moon endures;
turn but twice
and the ice
will blanch the morning at your doors.

EAT IT ALL UP, DARLINGS

The Great Consumer
crops the ground bare
where are the flowers?
Where the sweet parsnip?

Over Barren
over Sorry
he hovers
he scours

Where are the ape and
the leopard?
where the juicy pigs?

The rivers are tarmacked over
the fish have emigrated
the bees committed
collective suicide

Earth the brown loaf
is eaten to the last slice
the sea is a rude squelch at the end of the straw
at the very bottom of the glass....

The Great Consumer now
flaps black wings
peers at the crumbs in the sky

TALES

Tall tales
high as the mast,
pieces of gale
the sailor brought home from sea.

Small tales
carried in grandmother's
pocket, in the flowered
apron of time. Strands of bright wool.

Pretty tales
told to plain children:
once there was
Good Luck and Good Luck won;

And married Good Looks
and they begot Good Nature.
Happy princes!
They're living yet.

FRAGMENT

My father lifted
a mouthorgan up
to the wind on a hill

and the wind of Bohemia
sighed a few
frail and blue notes

man and child
in a harebell light
frail ghosts....faint tune

PAPER BOAT

Make a little paper boat,
Take it to the river,
If it swims and stays afloat,
You will live forever.

BANG

When the goodies are all gone
what shall we do
with the old brown bag of an earth
but blow it up - BANG

Crumpled brown paper bag
scuttling along
the desolate white
lanes of the universe

TOAD

Toads, toads, your place is full of them
you complain, & what do I see
but a small toad slip from your mouth &

HOp   HOp

over your beer & onto the floor
I ignore it the way one does

But how do I ignore
the vast stonecoloured toad in the centre of my house
where you deposited it where you spat it out
it sits   it sits
ancient and unshiftable
two thousand   murderous   years in weight

THE BIRTHRIGHT

Death is your birthright, guard it well.
(In these days, even death's uncertain.)
Some Clever-Dick could put the hurt on
Eternally - which would be hell.

Seventyseven years should serve
For feats of love, for feasts of blood:
For wickedness, for doing good,
Death is no more than we deserve.

THREE AUTUMNS IN REGENT'S PARK

The footballers
dance in the mist;
it muffles their shouts;
in muted colours
they rise
through the mist
through the trees.

      And once again
      the high stem of my heel
      roots in the damp
      leaf-mould for conkers-
      too late.

      Can't you remember-
      your father threw sticks for them
      and you carried them all off-
      years ago....

Under a tree
St Francis
in an old mac
preaches sermons
to the birds
from a crumpled brown
paper bag.

A LION, A WOLF AND A FOX

Stoatley Rough, Haslemere, 1942-1944

I went to school in a forest where I was taught
By a lion, a wolf and a fox.
How the lion shone! As he paced across the sky
We grew brown-limbed in his warmth and among the green leaves.

The fox was a musician. O cunning magician you lured
A small stream from its course with your *Forellenlied*,
Teaching it Schubert; and made the children's voices
All sound like early morning and auguries for a fine day.

Now the wolf was a poet and somewhat grey and reserved,
Something of a lone wolf – thoughts were his pack;
There was a garden in that forest, walled with climbing roses,
Where we would sit or lie and hear the wolf recite.

And sometimes we would listen, and sometimes the voice
Would turn into sunlight on the wall or into a butterfly
Over the grass. It was the garden of poetry and so
Words would turn into flowers and trees into verse.

This morning I received the grey pelt of a wolf,
And the fox and the lion write they are growing old;
That forest lies many years back, but we were in luck
To pass for a spell through that sunny and musical land.

OLD MRS LAZIBONES

(For Children)

Old Mrs Lazibones
And her dirty daughter
Never used soap
And never used water.

Higgledy piggledy cowpat
What d'you think of that?

Daisies from their fingernails,
Birds' nests in their hair-O,
Dandelions from their ears, -
What a dirty pair-O!

Higgledy piggledy cowpat
What d'you think of that?

Came a prince who sought a bride,
Riding past their doorstep,
Quick, said Mrs Lazibones.
Girl, under the watertap.

Higgledy piggledy cowpat
What d'you think of that?

Washed her up and washed her down,
Then she washed her sideways,
But the prince was far, far away,
He'd ridden off on the highways.

Higgledy piggledy cowpat
What d'you think of that?

SHALLOW POEM

I've thought of a poem.
I carry it carefully,
nervously, in my head,
like a saucer of milk;
in case I should spill some lines
before I can put it down.

THE KNOCKABOUT SHOW

The knockabout show
is over for the day;
candyfloss & toffeeapple
are licked to the bone;
and the moon shines over the sea,
and the moon shines over the sea,
and the little waves are
silver fish.

Punch & Judy,
deflated now, sleep;
abandoned,
arms thrown around each other.

The devil is nursing
the bump on his head;
the copper has turned
the corner;
against an old-fashioned lamp-post
Toby the dog
is raising a thoughtful leg.

ALL THE LEAVES HAVE LOST THEIR TREES

(For Hannah who said it)

All the leaves have lost their trees.
Child, what tumbled words are these?
(Yet I grieve for my lost tree:
Far away the wind bore me.)

LULLABY

Go to sleep, the moon in amber
Still is guardian of your slumber,

Or at least makes out to be
A symbol of serenity.

Though we have been fooled before,
Still, we greet him and turn o'er;

Pleased to think that for this night
We are watched by a fair light.

A MATTER OF TASTE

It is good taste to have
good taste in
pictures, furniture, dress;
it is in bad taste to worry
whether your pictures, dress,
furniture,
are in good taste or not...
Don't talk about taste, you snob.

It is in good taste
always and always
to consume good books.
The Good Book, however,
in not
in the best of taste.

It is in the worst of all
possible tastes to
speak about
money, politics, sex, or
religion; - further,
do not speak of yourself,
that's egotistical;
don't speak about others
in gossip;
do not question him, her,
about himself or herself:
don't pry.
You may speak of the theatre, -
but not to the housebound;
of concerts,
but not to the deaf.

Do not speak of your ailments,
which, if small, are absurd:
shocking, when great.

Don't speak of your
children, grandchildren,
waistline &
pets, & don't
speak of the
weather, - we've
had all these topics
before.

Do not speak of food
when at table;
that is in bad taste.
And don't
ask for *Daddies Sauce*
to put on your taties.

Is taste subjective?
Is it a matter of fashion?
Are there eternal
laws about taste, such as:
NOTHING TOO MUCH?

All I know finally is
that my taste is good,
your taste is *terrible*, - but
to pretend otherwise
is good taste on my part.

HIDE AND SEEK

Once I used to hide
in the open recess
under the first
floor balcony,
(*and always,*
my father remarked,
in the same place).

Where can she be?
Where can she be?
Here comes my aunt
searching and thin
and walks past me the first time;
this being the ritual.

Forty years later
and the recess
has shrunk to
under my chin;
and is full of
old lumber now and
a better place to hide in.
I look into the shadows
and ask and ask
where are they?

SAGE

If you are slightly bored, you are in luck,
and should not ask the gods to organise
too long an outing from the days you dwell in;
such prayers have a knack of being heard,
and exile is a hard land to do well in.

The guru spoke - and from experience.
And yawned. And wished himself ten bolts of
    thunder hence.

BASHO TRIES AGAIN

Luminous flutter
of wings over grass. Oh - a
cellophane wrapper!

X MARX THE SPOT

I puff at a dandelion.
Sorry, Harpo!

DANDELIONS

Such brazen slatterns:
but later, whitehaired, genteel.

TO A CONKER

Glossy horse-chestnut
foal, if you do not today
fall on luck &
found a horse-
chestnut tree, tomorrow
will have you defeated,
meagre, matt-coated,
unsheltered, shrunk, bony-ribbed, and , perhaps,
tied to a string; - so
land on Good Luck; conquer!

THE INHERITOR

I the sophisticated primate
Have stunted fingers on my feet,
And almost I control my climate,
And Everything is what I eat.

I wrote the story of Creation
When I discovered nudity:
The world is yours for exploitation.
I gave this charter unto me.

I traded in for my survival
My peaceful heart, my flealined coat;
Outpaced my vegetarian rival.
I have Creation by the throat.

WHITE LAMPLIGHT

Why is the night sky rosy at the edges
and over the rooftops?
Is it the breath of lamplight,
small and apricot in the distance but,
in the side-street here, white,
flowering on tall stalks?

The street of bungalows
takes on a holiday air
it is so at ease;
its various blunders are hidden.
I sit by the empty milkbottles
under a silken moon
and watch the white lamps flower.

At dawn their petals will drop
leaving stamens of delicate mauve.

FAREWELL

Forty years burying them
(there were so many);
but the ground is covered,
the words engraved,
the flowers are sown:
Farewell.

And I'm suddenly
tired of death &
mourning. But where
is there left to go
except to my own dark?

Light up the
cooker to warm
your buttocks, old woman.
The black cat will
lick himself, the clock go
tick tock. Time for the sad
cosy interlude now
before it is time
to climb up to bed.

TIME WATCHING

In a dark bar at the Rose and Crown
Where the poets are gathered (the aspiring poets!)
'What is the nature of time?' asks one.
'If time has no end,
Then time
Can have had no beginning.
Therefore there is no *Time*.'
TIME, cries the landlord.
We troop out, disperse,
And catch the last bus home.

'Have you read Thomas Mann?'
She asks. 'Time, he says,
Is subjective. A brief moment
Sharply remembered expands
In the mind; many days, many years,
Of what is repeated, shrink retrospectively.'
(Has your life been short? What happened
To all the time in the world?)

Time is essentially change.
We turn into old women
Before we've stopped laughing at them.
                                        Yet —

Tomorrow, tomorrow, we say
Wishing time away...
Garland me with tomorrow.

Whether or not it will all be the same
In a hundred years, in a million
It assuredly will be. Therefore,
Sleep easy, my heart.

But the darkness laments;
And the heart, unsettled,
Beats a quite different tempo
Of quick concern.
'Bad times. Bad times.'

HOUSE MOVING

Our bodies shed dust
and renew themselves.

What are our ghosts in old haunts
except a wraith of dust?

Time, the new owner, comes bringing
bucket and mop along, a fresh coat of paint.

THE MAN ON THE DESERT ISLAND (5)

The man on the desert island
Has taken a winter cruise;
Around and around the island –
He wants to surprise himself.

But what can he hope to find?
Some rosy shell, perhaps,
Like the fingernail of the goddess
Who goes cruising on other shores;

Or driftwood from the big ship
That never came his way...
His thoughts become postcard-sized.
He'll read them when he gets home.

NOAH

(For Children)

When Noah sailed the wet and blue
he took in the animals two by two.

When the animals made too much of a din,
There was water without, but wine within.

The bulls they bellowed, the ducks made quack,
The geese went honk, but Noah lay back.

The cuckoo went cuckoo, the owls went hoot,
Mrs Noah said much, but Noah stayed mute.

And Noah lay in his hammock all day,
While the ark continued its watery way.

The dogs cried woof, but the cat gave a purr,
Because Ham, Shem and Japheth, were stroking his fur.

Ham slipped up, but his brothers were nifty,
And Noah lived on to nine hundred and fifty.

ESMERALDA

Esmeralda in the nude
Went to open the front door.
This, of Esmerald' was rude,
As she had been told before.
And to make it even ruder,
He who'd knocked came in and scruder.

DULL TOWN...

Dull town, my beloved,
I bid you farewell.
What does destiny look like?
Only hindsight can tell.

Who here will recall me
when I have gone?
Go ask the mirror,
Forty years on.

GOD WOT

"A garden is a lovesome thing, God Wot!"-
T.E.Brown

Left over from the Flower-arranging class,
Stuck in a jar donated by Pottery,
They pose before us, wilting, a sorry bunch.
We dip the brush for some God-Wottery.

Mabel and Barbara dutifully attempt
To paint them for the lovesome things they
    were,
To me they're in a carriage pointing East,
And wave thin hands, and fight for the fetid
    air.

The tulip's ripped, the wallflower underfoot,
But I lack the talent and nerve to portray
    them thus:
Though I know their names; though I know
    their faces and names.
Forgetmenot, you're rendered anonymous.

W.H.Auden,
Much as I admire
All your philosophic-
Al thoughts upon the john,
Yet I'll take this chance to
Make good your omission:
You forgot to mention
Sir John Harington.

In 1589 he
Invented the contraption
You and I and others
Have liked to muse upon.
Praise to the creator,
To a fellow poet
To a fellow-mover,
Praise to good Sir John.

MY OWN MY NATIVE LAND...

That's it –
the house at the back –
home of my childhood.
The bloomers hung out to dry
in what once was the daisyfield
have been added since.
Unabashed they flaunt themselves
well to the fore.
A flag hoisted by the usurpers, they say:
Seeker of the past – this is new land.

FOR TOMMY

First there's Doubting Thomas.
What he wants is
irrefutable proof,
even if it means
probing your wound with his finger.
We respect him in theory.
We wish he'd leave off.

Then there's Thomas the Thief,
son of the piper.
He's broken into the piggy bank
and made off with the contents.
Bad Thomas! In Africa
they beat Tom-Toms.

'Tom, Dick and Harry
were three fine men.'
When I was young
I loved them all.
But it was Tom I loved first.

There are so many Thomases.
Wales abounds in them.
Every Welsh poet is a Thomas.
But Thomas the Rhymer was Scotch.

Thomas Stearns Eliot
once wrote a play
about Thomas A Becket.
When Thomas A Becket died
he was holy but verminous.

And Tommy went for a soldier.
He lies in a foreign field.
And his headstone says,
Known to God.
True Thomas!

And speaking of Toms,
there's my old tom cat:
he of the loving heart
and the gashed ear.

Uncle Tom's in bad odour
though he moved a world in his day:
but Uncle Tom Cobbley and all
is a good song still...

When you are old, you will say,
poor Tom's a-cold, or
more people know Tom Fool
than Tom Fool knows, -
when the little boys hoot in the street.

THE LODGER

I used to live all by myself
Like a rusty tea caddy on a shelf.

My head is bald, I'm an old crone,
I used to live by myself alone.

And ROOM TO LET the window said,
But no one creaked on the iron bed.

At the end of the year a stranger came,
He took the room, he gave no name.

He is silent and sly, he is up to no good,
He looks through chinks as no gentleman should;

He has hidden the gold-edged chamberpot,
He has been at the cheese, he takes the lot.

No use to hide anything or lock it,
He has pinched the only bulb from its socket!

One day, when I lie chill in my bed,
He will put the pillow over my head,

Pull down the blinds, switch off the day,
Pocket my eyes and walk away.

CARVE ME UP WHEN I DIE

Carve me up when I die
I bestow myself
on these various places:

My skull to my dentist
so that my full
set of teeth
may beam its
thanks on him.

My heart shall be placed
under the brick
by the rose,
to join Pip my cat.

Put my hands in a muff
somewhere under the
lazy daisies.
They shall be
bone idle.

Bury my tongue and my ears
well away from each other:
so that my ears
need not be afflicted
by the tale of my life
told over by the tongue.

And put clay into my ears.
They above all wish to die
Let no sorrowing sound
reach them.

As for the rest of me,
let the sea have it.
Let it enjoy the sea.

Except for my feet.
Send them back into childhood.
Bury them in the garden there.

THE POETRY READING

She's all virgin ear and he's good-looking.
He reads; she squeals delight. Her body's rocking
In time to his tongue's rhythms. He, for once,
Is able to discern a sound response.
Her jeans splay out; her hand hangs somewhat near
Her third, instinctive, pulsing nether ear.
The other women in the circle fade
To a mere backdrop. Certainly she's made
His evening. 'Give us more,' she cries
When he folds up and makes as if to rise.
And he obliges; finally withdraws
To her loud SUPER! - and some pale applause.

ANON

I was resting my feet between two pogroms
And cooling them in a stream,
When through the tender leaves above
I saw an angel gleam.

My guardian angel: I knew him at once.
He floated about the tree.
Now carry me off and carry me high.
And he said *presently.*

And presently means by-and-by,
And by-and-by, anon.
He settled his halo and flapped his wings;
He kissed me and was gone.

MRS K's LETTER

Dear Sirs, I want to disinter
My deceased parents - him and her.

Could you locate them? Somehow I
Am not quite certain where they lie.

But shaken free of earth they'll be –
Perfectly good - restored to me.

I long for that. Please go and look
Into your cemetery book;

And, having found them, send me word
Without delay, care of this ward.

I hope to leave here and renew
My life with them. My thanks to you.

THE POET RECLINING

(Marc Chagall, 1915)

All poets dream of this: the rural retreat,
the meadow stained-glass, a piggy-bank in the background.
A horse standing for freedom. The simple life.

Who's minding the beanrows though? Who mucks the pig out?
Will the horse amble up to inspect him and slobber his face?
What if the neighbours (there's a fence) turn the radio up?

The sky is a dusky rose; night enters the trees.
He lies in a heartache of grass, it is so green.
Later, he'll saddle up and make for the Seine.

ON A SHEET OF FORMICA: AN INCANTATION

Troll-eyes in formica wood
On the kitchen-table-top;
Wounds where branches got the chop
Though mere semblance: who can tell
Whether such may be withstood;
Whether they bode ill or well.

Scientific art has here
In an artless way transferred
The all-ancient, the absurd.
Superstitious notions rise
To the surface. Half in fear
I observe those goblin eyes.

Ring on ring around those knots:
What a sorrowing gaze is cast,
As if from some gnarled past.
Laminated rustic kitsch,
There's a distant ground where rots
Leafmould growing dark and rich.

What I touch on is no kin
Of true wood. It works no charm,
Sylvan spell or elfin harm;
Yet it fills me with unease.
It invites the forest in
Seemingly. Befriend me, trees!

MAKE BELIEVE

Say I were not sixty,
say you weren't near-hundred,
say you were alive.
Say my verse was read
in some distant country,
and say you were idly turning the pages:

The blood washed from your shirt,
the tears from your eyes,
the earth from your bones;
neither missing since 1940,
nor dead as reported later
by a friend of a friend of a friend...

Quite dapper you stand in that bookshop
and chance upon my clues.

That is why at sixty
when some publisher asks me
for biographical details,
I still carefully give
the year of my birth
the name of my hometown:

GERDA MAYER born '27, in Karlsbad,
Czechoslovakia...write to me, father.

NOTE: The author's father, Arnold Stein, escaped from the German concentration camp in Nisko in 1939, fled to Russian-occupied Lemberg/Lwow, and then disappeared in the summer of 1940. It is thought he may have died in a Russian camp.

LINES WRITTEN IN HIGH DARREN, LLANIGAN, NEAR HAY-ON-WYE, 1980

Outside upon a large green mat
My Sunday-dinner's getting wet.

Without a mac, without a brolly,
No wonder sheep look melancholy.

I stop my step and speak them fair;
The young ones, true, return my stare,

Twitch ears, when I begin to praise
Their winsome, white and woolly ways.

The older ones move from their station.
They're wise beyond their reputation.

Though bland my visage, soft my roar,
They spot in me the carnivore;

The sentimental salivator,
The cardiganned commiserator,

And turn. How is it that mere lamb
Sees me the monster that I am?

THE SEVEN

AVARICE had a bad childhood
And thrift is her problem.
All her clobber's in rags;
She can't spare the thread for the mending.

Once LUST at his best
Was coarsely benevolent:
Now his largesse
Aids we don't know whom.

WRATH rattles the cage of ribs
And bellows for his release.
Deny him too long
And he'll chew up your heart.

PRIDE's a proper gentleman.
How was he ever confounded
With his brother Purseproud, his cousin Disdain,
His servile son Snob?

GLUTTONY, big booby, except in hard times
Why should anyone mind you?
You simply like a lot. Your cholesterol level
Is surely your own affair.

SLOTH, you slattern,
You slippered scandal, you frump,
The other housewives make beds, jams, doilies.
(Amazing how careworn their faces.)

You envy them all, ENVY.
You've told me again and again
That whatever they say to the contrary
You are the worst off.

THE CRUNCH

(For Children)

The lion and his tamer
They had a little tiff,
For the lion limped too lamely, –
The bars had bored him stiff.

No call to crack your whip, Sir!
Said the lion then irate:
No need to snap my head off,
said the tamer - but too late.

POPLAR

propped up
against the pale
wall of the sky,
small birds
snipped from
black paper
pose there
in silhouette:
summer's dark plume is
winter's besom broom

MALE BUTTERFLIES COURT FALLING LEAVES

Male butterflies court falling leaves
And male frogs mount galoshes;
Nature exuberantly sways
In dingy mackintoshes;

Or plugs itself into some wild
Or odd sex-aiding symbol,
In desperate hilarity,
In deeply-earnest gambol.

Love has a bash. It needn't end
In flower, fruit or future:
There's profligacy, waste; there is
The seediness of nature.

CONFETTI

Pelted by
flowering cherry, the sterile
elderly couple
sweeten themselves in the sun.
A blue-eyed Sunday in May. So
bountiful a confetti
they know
must result in luck.

OWL

How mournfully the owl hoots
And who can tell what it denotes:
Across the dusk he sounds to me
Like the last owl on the last tree.

CHILDREN WITH CANDLES

The children are the candles white,
Their voices are the flickering light.

The children are the candles pale,
Their sweet song wavers in the gale.

Storm, abate! Wind, turn about!
Or you will blow their voices out.

GRANDFATHER'S HOUSE

Grandfather's house rose up so tall,
Its steps were like a waterfall
It had a deep stairwell, as I recall.

And down the banisters slid my mother,
And her sisters, and her brother,
And many a child, many another.

The banisters wobbled and down fell all.
Down, down, down, and beyond recall.
And so I was not born at all.

Better it is not to have been,
Than to have seen what I have seen.
So deck their graves with meadow-green.

THE FART OF AN ANGEL

The fart of an angel as everyone knows
Has the fragrance of violets, the scent of a rose.
The burps are all birdsong, the flesh is all spirit,
And those are the ways I intend to inherit.
And when I drift past you and murmur *Beg Pardon*,
You'll deem all of heaven a blossoming garden.

ONCE

The cherub gooseberry, the angelic redcurrant,
enclosed the Garden of Paradise: they and the
flowering, pink white and golden
choir of heavenly shrubs. Beyond
lay the world of forest and fairy of
hobgoblin bilberries, dainty wildstrawberries,
blackberries, raspberries. We
one-time-gatherers now scour the wood
for the last on the branch: before the sparse winter.

ABSORBED

As the customer struggles
into the shoe
the salesgirl sidles
towards the looking glass.
The mirror absorbs her
into a dream of herself.

CINDERELLA'S SLIPPER

The magical foot:
so small, so white, so yielding,
that the glass slipper
will fit no other.

Cosmetic surgery
with the kitchen knife
will not avail here.
There'll be tell-tale signs.

As for the slipper,
it is ensconced in a fairy tale
and forever on display:
glass behind glass;

And a solace to old Cinders
now hobbling to answer
the bungalow doorbell
when the chiropodist calls.

*In the Grimm version of 'Cinderella' each of the Ugly Sisters
cuts off part of her foot (one her toes, the other her heel)
to make it fit the slipper.*

THE EMIGRATION GAME —
WINTER 1938/39

Mother and I walk through the streets of Prague.
Her hands are balled against the falling snow.
(Can't she afford gloves? Are they bare from choice?)
There's snow above and endless steps below.

We have a bag of chocolate-creams; we play
The Emigration Game: England, if brown;
Or, if the centre's white, we must stay here;
If yellow, it's Australia. Snow falls down.

I pick a brown and mother has the white.
She walks with a straight back: let's try again.
Her legs are varicosed; her heels are raised.
She's bearing up and stout of heart. In vain

From consulate to consulate her steps
Inscribe petitions. Soon the sweets are gone.
Then March comes and invaders bar all routes:
Yet leave no trace of her when they move on;

Their footsteps beating time and bearing down.

MIRRORS

How solemn they look,
how intent, the young women
in self-appraisal...

AT NIGHT

The homely empties
wait on the doorstep. The lamplight touches them up.

STOCK STILL

(For Children)

There was a woman who stood stock-still
in the middle of the street.
"Shall I go shopping today," she said,
"and buy some things to eat
for a treat
or shall I go home again," she said,
"and make do with whatever there is to be had?"

The shops they shut and opened again,
and shut and opened once more;
her husband came home and went out again,
and came back, and went out through the door.
And still the woman stood in the street
and went neither to nor fro.
"There's not much point in moving," she said,
"Till I know which way to go."

So long she stood, so much engrossed,
she's turned into a sign-post.

FORESTS ARE FELLED TO MAKE ANTHOLOGIES IN PRAISE OF FORESTS IN DEFENCE OF TREES

Forests are felled to make anthologies
In praise of forests; in defence of trees.

DULLARD-THE-MIND: SLUGGARD-THE-BODY

Dullard-the-Mind and Sluggard-the-Body
Look at the time and it stands at unholy;

Look at the hour, which has stopped at unkind.
'What's to be done?' asks Dullard-the-Mind.

But Sluggard-the-Body shuffles to catch
The last cooling lunch at the serving hatch.

SWIMMER'S SONG

On this grey deserted sea,
Every wave has lifted me.
As I love and claim the water,
Surely I am Neptune's daughter.
If I drowned, I'd have it known
He has recognised his own.

GIPSY SONG

In fog, in drizzle, in heavy snow,
In the wilds of the forest, in the wintering night,
I heard the hungerhowls of the wolves,
I heard the owls cry.
> Waily wow wow wow!
> Waily wo wo wo!
> Witoohoo!

Once I shot at a cat on top of a fence;
It was Anne-the-witch's - her dear black cat.
At night from the village there came to me
Seven of the werewolves, seven-seven women.
> Waily wow wow wow!
> Waily wo wo wo!
> Witoohoo!

I knew them all I knew them well,
Katy, Annie, Ursula,
Barbs and Beth, Eve and Liz.
They made a circle and howled at me.
> Waily wow wow wow!
> Waily wo wo wo!
> Witoohoo!

So I called them loudly by their names:
What is it, Anne? What is it, Beth?
They rocked themselves, they shook themselves,
And ran and howled away.
> Waily wow wow wow!
> Waily wo wo wo!
> Witoohoo!

Goethe (1749-1832)
translated from the German by Gerda Mayer

HUNGER

Hunger: it waits for days, perhaps for years.
Look, this is how. Hold it the right way up.
Then food descends from heaven and you eat up.

The little hand has scraped the bowl and crammed
the food into the mouth as best it could.
The bowl is empty now. The food was good.

The child attempts the magic formula
again. Turns the bowl over and then up.
The bowl stays empty and the day is up.

The bowl is empty and his day is up.

MALHAM TARN FIELD CENTRE – YORKSHIRE, 1992

The full moon stands above the tarn
And sees three moons reflected there;
Shadowy rabbits dance the sward,
The midges fidget in the air;
Across the lake a single note:
A curlew calls into the night.
The larches, dark on darkening air,
Are like a curtain drawn apart
To show the moon above the tarn
That sees three moons reflected there.

TWO HAIKU

Autumn Soltitude:
A tree framed in the window;
The glow of old books.

* * * * *

After the dark rain,
A fragrant May moon:
The blossom all-moon-entangled.

THE MISANTHROPE'S BABY POEM

I look at them, if look I must:
I view them with benign disgust.

I see them with disguised dismay;
And do I covet them? - No way!

My own would have improved the nation.
Yours make for overpopulation.

Parental Pride, do not suppose
I like them much beyond their toes.

I very cheerfully dispense
With whiffs of their incontinence.

They have one single merit - that's
Being a substitute for cats.

Have they a sex? The only clues
Are puky pinks and bilious blues.

What is their weather? Wet and windy.
Their yowling makes a dismal shindy.

They're boring, bawling, bandy, bald.
I straight forget what they are called.

How's Baby? Whey - and pudding -faced;
Uncalled for proof that you've embraced.

I'd not have doubted it. A letter -
French - dropped my way would have done better.

For every Jack, for every Janet,
Commiserations, luckless Planet!

KAFFEE UND KUCHEN

For Martin Bax

Five monumental ladies, in dark stuffs,
Are wedged around the table's festive gloom:
My step-grandmother and four birthday guests,
Above the grocery shop, in a small room.
        No paper hats, balloons, or floral frocks,
        No strawberry ices, no white ankle-socks.

That's Arnold's child. A cursory, polite,
Inspection follows. Fustily sedate
They sit and sip. The air is full of crumbs.
They place a slice of tombstone on my plate.
        How could I know my dainty limbs would grow
        As mountainous as theirs, - my heart as low?

Did my arrival spoil some party game
Of cosy confidences? Happiness
Is largely relative. (Worse may befall and will.)
Perhaps they thought their party a success.
        Pop the champagne! Prise open lemonades!
        Set out the coffee cups. Here's to their shades.